STECK-VAUGHN

WINNERS

NOBEL PRIZE

Melissa Stone Billings

Henry Billings

STECK-VAUGHN®
COMPANY

Books in this series:

Congressional Medal of Honor
Halls of Fame
Olympic Games
Nobel Prize

Acknowledgments

Executive Editor
Elizabeth Strauss

Photo Editor
Margie Foster

Production and Design
Howard Adkins Communications

Cover Illustration
Linda Adkins Design

Illustration Credits
Gary McElhaney

Photo Credits
P.2 The Bettmann Archive; p.4 The Bettmann Archive; p.7 The Bettmann Archive; p.10 UPI/Bettmann; p.12 AP/Wide World; p.14 AP/Wide World; p.15 The Library of Congress; p.18 The Bettmann Archive; p.19 The Bettmann Archive; p.20 UPI/Bettmann; p.21 UPI/Bettmann; p.24 AP/Wide World; p.25; p.26. AP/Wide World; p.27 UPI/Bettmann; p.30 UPI/Bettmann; p.31 UPI/Bettmann; p.32 UPI/Bettmann; p.34 © G. Mendel/Magnum; p.35 © G. Mendel/Magnum; p.38 UPI/Bettmann; p.39 The Bettmann Archive; p.41 UPI/Bettmann; p.44 AP/Wide World; p.45 AP/Wide World; p. 47 AP/Wide World; p.48 UPI/Bettmann; p.49 UPI/Bettmann; p.52 UPI/Bettmann; p.55 UPI/Bettmann; p.56 UPI/Bettmann; p.60 Reuters/Bettmann; p.62 AP/Wide World; p.63 Rick Williams; p.66 AP/Wide World; p.68 UPI/Bettmann; p.69 UPI/Bettmann; p.72 AP/Wide World; p.74 AP/Wide World; p.76 AP/Wide World; p.80 Reuters/Bettmann; p.81 Reuters Bettmann; p.82 AP/Wide World; p.83 AP/Wide World.

ISBN 0-8114-4781–2

The Nobel Prize

The Nobel Prize is named after Alfred Nobel, a Swedish inventor. Nobel made a fortune from his invention of dynamite, but he was worried about how dynamite would be used in the future. In his will, he set up the Nobel Prizes. He wanted his money to go to men and women who helped humankind. The Nobel Prizes are given in six areas: literature, peace, medicine, chemistry, physics, and economics. The Nobel Prizes are awarded each year on December 10, the day that Alfred Nobel died. The prizes were first given in 1901. Each prize winner receives a gold medal, a diploma, and a large sum of money.

Contents

Marie Curie

Two-Time Winner

University
a school of higher learning

interrupted
broke in while someone else was speaking

education
training for a job

Marie sat at the breakfast table with her brother and her two sisters. She listened closely as Joseph talked about his life as a student at the **University** of Warsaw.

But something was bothering Marie. Finally she **interrupted** her brother. "I'm happy for you, Joseph. But what about Bronya and me? How will we get an **education**? Women aren't allowed into the university."

Joseph grew quiet. "I know. It's not fair. If only we had more money. Then you could go to another country to study."

The Deal

Marie Sklodowska knew that her close, talented family didn't have much money. For Joseph and Hela it wouldn't be such a problem. Joseph could study to become a doctor while living at home.

Hela planned to be a singer. But Marie and Bronya needed money to follow their dreams. Both girls wanted an education. Without the money to leave Poland, they would never get it.

Ever since their mother had died in 1878, Bronya had taken care of the family. Like Marie, Bronya had done well in school. She longed to go to Paris where she could study to become a doctor. "There must be some way to get Bronya to Paris," Marie thought. "Then maybe, someday, I can go, too."

At last Marie had an idea. "I'll make a deal with you," she told Bronya. "I'll get a job here in Poland. The money that you have saved and what I earn will be enough to send you to the university in Paris."

Bronya could not believe her ears. "You can't mean it!" she said.

Marie Curie went to the Sorbonne University in Paris.

But Marie answered, "Yes, I do mean it. We can both keep working on our own. But then neither one of us will get away. This way we can both get an education. After you become a doctor, it will be my turn. You will give me money so that I can study in Paris."

Bronya's eyes filled with tears. Her sister's plan would make her dream come true. "Why should I go first?" she asked at last. "You are at least as smart as I am."

"Don't be silly," answered Marie. "You are twenty years old and I am only seventeen. I've got lots of time. It is only right that you go first. Believe me, this is our best chance. My plan will work!"

Hard Times

And so Bronya went off to Paris to study. Marie got a job caring for the children of a rich Warsaw

Pierre and Marie Curie

family. During this time Marie was lonely and unhappy. It seemed that the five years would never pass. She borrowed library books and tried to teach herself science. But in a letter to a cousin she wrote, "My life is that of a prisoner."

At last Marie's five years were over. In 1891, she joined Bronya in Paris. At first she lived in Bronya's apartment. But she needed peace and quiet for her studies, so she decided to get a place of her own.

Marie couldn't afford a good apartment so she moved into a tiny, unheated room. She barely had enough to eat. A few times Marie was so weak that she fainted in class. Still, she managed to finish first in her class in 1893.

Marie and Pierre

In 1894, Marie fell in love with a young scientist named Pierre Curie. Pierre was already well-known in his field. He and his brother, Jacques, had made important discoveries about electricity. To show his love, Pierre did not send Marie flowers. He sent her papers he had written. Marie thought, "Here is someone who loves science as much as I do." On July 25, 1895, she and Pierre were married.

The 1890's were an exciting time for the Curies. Scientists were learning new things everyday. One of the most important discoveries was made by Henri Becquerel. He found out that a metal called **uranium** gave off special rays. These rays were called **radiation**. Marie decided to study radiation. Her work captured Pierre's interest. He gave up his own **research** to help her in her work.

To get the uranium they needed, Marie and Pierre used a kind of rock called pitchblende.

uranium
a metal that gives off special rays

radiation
energy that is given off in waves

research
careful study of a certain subject

Each piece of pitchblende had a different amount of uranium. One day in 1898, they came across a strange piece of pitchblende. It gave off a huge amount of radiation.

"Look at this!" cried Marie. "These rays can't all be coming from the uranium!" The Curies looked at each other. There had to be something else that was giving off rays. But what was it?

Marie and Pierre broke the pitchblende into small pieces. They took out the uranium. Still the pitchblende gave off rays. Finally they had only a speck of black powder. This speck gave off 400 times as many rays as uranium. The Curies called this new **element** "polonium." The name was in honor of Poland, Marie's home country. Marie and Pierre also found a second new element in pitchblende. This one they called "radium." It gave off 1000 times as many rays as uranium.

Dangerous Work

Marie and Pierre knew they had made important discoveries. But they didn't have enough polonium or radium to test. "We need more," said Pierre. "We need a lot more." They paid to have a **ton** of pitchblende shipped to them. Together the two scientists worked in a cold, leaky shed. Marie wrote, "It was in this **miserable** old shed that the best and happiest years of our life were spent." Although no one knew it at the time, this work was very dangerous. The rays from polonium and radium were deadly.

At last after four years, they had enough radium to weigh and test. In 1903, the Curies, along with Henri Becquerel, won the Nobel Prize in **Physics**. The prize honored them for their work with

element
one kind of matter

ton
2,000 pounds

miserable
run-down

Physics
science of matter and energy

Marie Curie working in her laboratory.

uranium. For Marie this moment had special meaning. It was the first time a woman had ever won a Nobel Prize.

Three years later, Pierre Curie was killed in a traffic accident. Marie was heartbroken, but she went on with her work. In 1911, she won a second Nobel Prize. This one was for the discovery of polonium and radium. In 1934, at the age of 66, Marie Curie died. The long years of working with radiation had finally cost her life.

Vocabulary Skill Builder

■ Write the best word to complete each sentence. Use each word only once.

research	uranium	radiation	elements

Marie Curie spent many years studying a metal called

(1)_____ . This metal gave off (2)_____ .

Marie also discovered two new (3)_____ "radium"

and "polonium." Marie's (4)_____ won her two

Nobel Prizes.

■ Match each word with its meaning.

_____ **1.** interrupted   **a.** a school of higher learning

_____ **2.** university   **b.** run-down

_____ **3.** ton   **c.** the study of matter and energy

_____ **4.** miserable   **d.** began talking before someone else finished speaking

_____ **5.** education   **e.** knowledge

_____ **6.** physics   **f.** 2,000 pounds

Read and Remember

■ Place a check mark (✔) in front of three things that Marie Curie did.

_____ 1. Marie Curie invented uranium.

_____ 2. Marie Curie worked for five years so that her sister could go to school.

_____ 3. Marie Curie spent years studying radiation.

_____ 4. Marie Curie married a doctor.

_____ 5. Marie Curie won two Nobel Prizes.

_____ 6. Marie Curie was killed in a traffic accident.

Write Your Ideas

■ Imagine you are Marie Curie. Write a letter to your brother explaining why you enjoy working in the cold, leaky shed in your backyard.

Dear Joseph,

_____

_____

_____

_____

_____

_____

_____

_____

_____

Albert Einstein

Poor Student, Great Thinker

The young girl giggled as the parade came into view. There were flags, horses, and marching soldiers. "Isn't it exciting, Albert?" she called to her brother.

Young Albert Einstein didn't say anything. But he looked as if he were about to cry. "What's the matter?" asked his sister with alarm.

"I feel sorry for those soldiers," Albert said. "Officers probably yell at them all the time. Being a soldier is just like being in school. And school is terrible!"

School Days

Albert Einstein was born in Germany on March 14, 1879. He didn't learn to speak for a long time. His parents worried that something might be wrong with him. Even after he learned to talk, Albert was different from most boys. He didn't enjoy the war games and sports that other boys his age liked. He spent much of his time alone with his own dreams and thoughts.

Things got worse when Einstein began going to school. At that time, German teachers were very **strict**. One day Einstein's uncle asked him about school. "I hate it," Einstein told him. "The teachers are mean. They yell at you if you don't **memorize** your lessons. Sometimes they beat you if you don't understand what the book says. But the worst part is they don't want anyone to ask questions."

Einstein wanted to make friends at school, but he found it hard. He was shy and spoke slowly. Most of his classmates thought he was stupid. The other boys rarely invited him to join their games. Often they teased him. They called him "Honest John" because he refused to lie even to keep from being punished.

By the time Einstein reached high school, he was very unhappy. He hated the way school was taught. All the teachers did was **drill**, drill, and more drill. Einstein was much more interested in finding out why and how things worked than in memorizing facts.

There were some things that Einstein did enjoy. He loved music. He could listen to great music for hours. He learned to play the violin when he was six years old. He even made up his own songs. Sometimes he played with grown-up musicians.

Einstein also liked **mathematics**. He often finished reading a math book before the rest of the class

strict
demanding

memorize
to learn by repeating many times

drill
to practice again and again

mathematics
the study of numbers

even began it. Mathematics made sense to Einstein because the problems could be solved step by step. He once said, "Mathematics is interesting because you can prove whether your answers are right or wrong. I like proving things."

New Chances

In 1895, the company run by Einstein's father failed. Hermann Einstein moved his family to Italy. There he opened a new business. Young Einstein was left in Germany to finish high school. He never made it.

After a few months, school **officials** encouraged the boy to leave. Surprised, Einstein asked one of his teachers why. The teacher said, "You didn't

officials
people in charge

Dr. Albert Einstein writes out an equation.

really break any rules, but you asked too many questions. You made the teachers look bad in front of the other students."

Einstein joined his family in Italy. At last he was happy. He took long walks in the mountains. He listened to music and went to museums. After a few months, he decided to try school in Switzerland. Swiss schools were not like German schools. The Swiss teachers helped and encouraged Einstein. He soon finished high school. Then he went on to college. His true gifts finally began to show.

When Einstein left school in 1900, he wanted to teach in a university. But he couldn't find a teaching job in Switzerland. So he took a job working in an office. The work wasn't hard, and it left him with plenty of free time. He was able to think about problems and write down his **conclusions**. He wrote a few papers and sent them to magazines. When these papers were printed, the 26-year-old Einstein became famous among scientists. Albert Einstein's ideas surprised and excited people because he looked at the world in a new way.

conclusions
opinions reached after thinking

Einstein's Ideas

One day Einstein spoke to a group of Americans about his ideas. He began by saying, "It is all very simple." Everyone laughed. No one except Einstein thought the ideas were simple. It took most people a long time to understand what he was talking about.

Before Einstein came along, people thought of most objects as **stationary**, or not moving. People believed that objects remained still until something

stationary
standing still

13

moved them. A ball in the middle of a pool table, for example, was not moving. It just sat there until it was hit by another ball. That seemed like common sense. But Einstein said that nothing is fixed. Everything is in motion. It all depends on how you look at it. To a person standing on the sun, the pool ball is moving. That's because the earth itself is moving around the sun.

In other words, everything is "**relative**." An elephant is big **compared** to a mouse. But an elephant is small compared to a mountain. A person on the seventh floor is "up" to someone on the second floor. But she is "down" to someone on the twelfth floor.

That part is easy. But Einstein also said that time is relative. To most people an hour is an hour. But Einstein said that time depends on speed. As you go faster, time slows down. A clock sitting on earth

relative
having meaning only when judged against something else

compared
checked to see how things are alike or different

Dr. Albert Einstein in his studio in Berlin in the early 1920s.

ticks away faster than a clock shooting through space in a spaceship. At low speeds the difference is hard to measure. But in a really fast spaceship the difference would be great. If a clock could travel at the speed of light—186,300 miles per second–it would not tick at all! Inside that spaceship, time would stand still.

Einstein also showed how a tiny bit of matter could be turned into a huge amount of **energy**. This idea explained how the sun could send out light and heat for millions of years without burning out.

energy
ability to do work

Albert Einstein became an American citizen in 1940.

Albert Einstein's ideas earned him the Nobel Prize in 1921. Today many people think that he was the greatest scientist who ever lived. That's not bad for someone who had trouble in school and was once thought of as "dull!"

Vocabulary Skill Builder

Part A

■ Write a paragraph using these three words from the story.

strict: insisting that all rules be carefully followed
mathematics: the study of numbers
drill: practice again and again

_____

_____

_____

_____

_____

Part B

■ Read each sentence. Fill in the circle next to the best meaning for the word in dark print. If you need help, use the Glossary.

1. Einstein believed that everything is **relative**.
   ○ a. not very good   ○ b. silly
   ○ c. meaningful only when judged with other things

2. The teachers yelled at him if he didn't **memorize** his lessons.
   ○ a. remember by heart   ○ b. write neatly   ○ c. speak out loud

3. The sun gives off a huge amount of **energy**.
   ○ a. practice   ○ b. time   ○ c. the ability to do work

4. Einstein **compared** time on Earth with time in a speeding spaceship.
   ○ a. worked with numbers   ○ b. painted a picture
   ○ c. looked to see what was the same and different

5. German school **officials** encouraged Einstein to leave.
   ○ a. people in charge   ○ b. students   ○ c. parents

6. He was able to write down his **conclusions**.
   ○ a. questions   ○ b. things not understood   ○ c. findings

7. Before Einstein, most people thought of objects as **stationary**.
   ○ a. hard to break   ○ b. expensive   ○ c. not moving

Read and Remember

■ Answer the questions.

1. Why did Albert Einstein feel sad when he watched the parade? _____

_____

2. Why did German teachers want Einstein to leave their school? _____

_____

3. How did Swiss teachers treat Einstein? _____

_____

4. Why did Einstein's ideas excite and surprise people? _____

_____

5. What would happen to a clock traveling at the speed of light? _____

_____

Think and Apply — Fact or Opinion?

■ Write **F** before each fact. Write **O** before each opinion.

_____ 1. Einstein had trouble making friends at school.

_____ 2. Einstein's German teachers were not very good.

_____ 3. Switzerland has the best teachers in all of Europe.

_____ 4. Einstein became famous when magazines printed his papers.

_____ 5. It is fun to learn mathematics.

_____ 6. The earth moves around the sun.

_____ 7. Einstein was given the Nobel Prize in 1921.

_____ 8. Einstein deserved to win two Nobel Prizes.

_____ 9. Einstein was the greatest scientist who ever lived.

_____ 10. An elephant is big compared to a mouse.

Alexander Fleming

Saving Millions

laboratory
scientist's workroom

medical
about medicine

Alexander Fleming leaned over his **laboratory** table. He frowned, staring at the results of his latest experiment. At the far end of the room, two **medical** students entered the lab. One of them noticed Fleming.

"Who is he?" the student asked.

"That's Dr. Fleming," the second student answered. "Poor guy. He's been working in this laboratory for almost twenty years. He keeps looking and looking for one certain thing, but he never finds it. He'll probably never find it . . ."

Looking for a Magic Bullet

Alexander Fleming did not hear the students' words that day in 1927. But it wouldn't have mattered if he had. Fleming didn't care what other people thought. This quiet Scottish scientist believed that some day his work would pay off. He planned to keep plugging away until that day came.

"What is it, exactly, that you are looking for?" a friend once asked Fleming.

"I'm looking for a new way to treat **infections**," Fleming replied. "A wound becomes infected when harmful **germs** enter your body. Your body's white blood **cells** will try to kill off these germs. If they succeed, you'll get better. If they fail, you'll get sicker and sicker. You may even die. I'm looking for a way to kill the germs that cause infections."

Fleming knew of several **drugs** that killed germs. But they also killed white blood cells. These drugs made sick people weaker. Fleming and others were looking for a "magic bullet"–a drug that would kill germs but not harm white blood cells.

infections
certain sicknesses

germs
tiny living things that can cause sicknesses

cells
bits of living matter

drugs
medicines

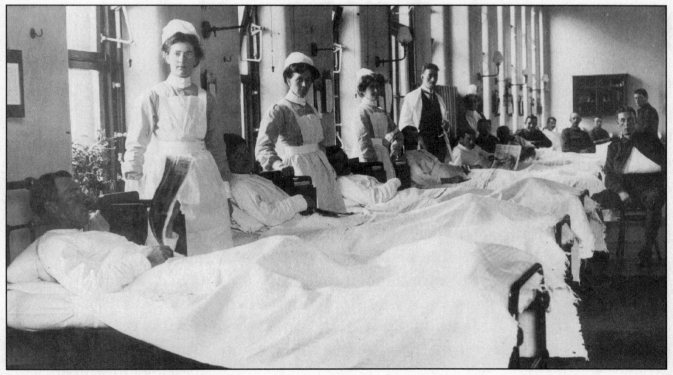

A hospital during World War I

Strange Habits

Fleming began working with germs in London in 1908. His life's work was interrupted only once. That was when World War I broke out in 1914. During the war Fleming served as an army doctor. He saw many soldiers die from infections. "It was **horrible**," he wrote, "to be surrounded by men who were suffering and dying without our being able to help them." When the war ended in 1918, Fleming returned to his lab. He came back more eager than ever to find a magic bullet.

horrible
terrible

Fleming holding penicillin mold

To many people, Fleming's work habits seemed strange. Most scientists were very neat. Each day they cleaned their **equipment**. Each night they threw out the things they no longer needed. Fleming, however, liked to wait two or three weeks before cleaning up. Often **mold** was growing in a dish before he threw it out. As it turned out, this habit would lead to the greatest discovery of his life.

equipment
supplies

mold
a furry growth

Fleming with G.I.s at Walter Reed Hospital

An Amazing Discovery

Fleming took a short vacation in 1928. As always, he left his work space a mess. Little glass dishes were lying all around. In these dishes were the germs Fleming had been studying. By the time Fleming returned, the dishes were moldy. Most people would have swept them into the garbage without a second glance. But Fleming looked carefully at each one. He noticed something strange in one dish. Spots of a rare, blue-green mold covered half the dish. To his surprise, there weren't any germs left in that part of the dish.

Had the mold killed the germs? Could this moldy liquid kill germs without harming white blood cells? After careful study, Fleming answered "yes" to both questions. He had finally found the magic bullet! He named it penicillin.

It took scientists twelve years to figure out how to use penicillin. At last they began using it to treat people with infections. In 1945, Alexander Fleming won the Nobel Prize for his discovery of this **miracle** drug. Penicillin would save millions of lives.

miracle
amazing

Vocabulary Skill Builder

■ Use the clues to complete the puzzle. Choose from the words in the box.

laboratory
medical
infections
cells
germs
drugs
horrible
equipment
mold
miracle

Across

5. having to do with medicine
6. medicines
7. an amazing thing
9. room where scientists do experiments
10. sicknesses caused when harmful things enter the body

Down

1. a furry growth
2. living things are made up of these
3. supplies
4. terrible
8. cause sicknesses

Read and Remember

■ Find the best ending for each sentence. Fill in the circle next to it.

1. Alexander Fleming wanted to
   ○ a. help sick people.   ○ b. make money.   ○ c. stop working.

2. As a scientist, Fleming was not very
   ○ a. smart.   ○ b. neat.   ○ c. hard working.

3. It took Fleming twenty years to
   ○ a. become an army doctor.   ○ b. make friends in London.
   ○ c. find the "magic bullet."

4. Fleming found penicillin growing in
   ○ a. his garden.   ○ b. his coffee cup.   ○ c. a glass dish.

5. Penicillin does not
   ○ a. hurt white blood cells.   ○ b. kill germs.   ○ c. save lives.

Write Your Ideas

■ Pretend you are Alexander Fleming. Write a short speech explaining why you are excited about your discovery of penicillin.

_____

_____

_____

_____

_____

_____

_____

_____

_____

Emily Greene Balch

Fighting for World Peace

*T*he messenger knocked on the door. "Come in," said Emily Greene Balch. She was sitting in her office at the Women's Congress in Switzerland. "The door's open."

"I have a letter for you from the United States," said the messenger.

The letter came from Ellen Pendleton, president of Wellesley College in Massachusetts. It was dated May 8, 1919. Balch opened the letter and began reading. "I'm sorry, Emily. The vote was close, but the officers have decided not to let you teach at Wellesley again."

A Stand for Peace

Emily Balch began teaching at Wellesley College in 1896. She became a teacher because she wanted to make the world a better place to live. For twenty years she taught that all people should be treated equally. She said, "People should be judged by what they do, not by their class, or race, or by whether they are a man or woman."

Balch acted on her ideas. She helped children from poor families. She fought for higher pay for workers. She called for better **conditions** for women workers.

In 1914, World War I broke out. Balch and 40 other American women went to Europe to develop a peace plan. They failed. In 1917, the United States joined the war. Balch thought the war was wrong. She thought *all* wars were wrong. Her ideas angered many Americans. Her beliefs even caused her to lose her teaching job at Wellesley. She was fired because of her "**outspoken** views on peace."

Balch tried to improve working conditions in factories.

A Private Struggle

During the 1930's, world peace was put in danger again. A new leader came to power in Germany. His name was Adolf Hitler. Hitler hated the Jewish people. He passed laws that made life very hard for German Jews. Some Jews left Germany. Balch helped dozens of these **refugees** find new homes in the United States.

refugees
people who are running away from danger

Balch receives a bouquet of flowers for her work on world wide peace.

In 1939, Hitler attacked Poland. That started World War II. Two years later, the United States entered the war. For Emily Balch, this was a terrible time. Night after night she lay in bed, unable to sleep. "What should I do?" she asked herself. "I have spent my whole life working for peace. I cannot support a war. Yet this is no ordinary war. Hitler is no ordinary enemy. . . ." Indeed, Hitler was an **evil** man. He wanted to take over the world. He was using death camps to kill a whole race of people.

Balch simply didn't know what to do. She later wrote, "I went through a long and **painful struggle** and never felt that I had reached a clear answer." In the end, she supported the war as best she could. She believed that someone had to stop Hitler. But her heart remained divided. She still thought war was a terrible waste. She hoped that one day people would learn to solve problems in a better way.

Helping Japanese-Americans

Japan was also America's enemy during World War II. Japan attacked Hawaii's Pearl Harbor on December 7, 1941. Many Americans blamed *all* Japanese people for the attack. That made life difficult for Americans with Japanese ancestors. The United States government made things even worse. In 1942, it forced over 100,000 Japanese-Americans to leave their homes. These people were sent to live in camps surrounded by **barbed-wire**. They were treated like **criminals** just because of their race.

Balch was very **concerned** about this unfair act. She worked to see that these people could one day return to friendly **communities**. She worked to see that they got money to cover part of what they had lost. Balch also sent puzzles and school supplies to the Japanese-American children in the camps.

World War II ended in 1945. The next year Emily Greene Balch won the Nobel Prize for Peace for her "lifelong work for the cause of peace."

evil
very bad

painful
causing hurt

struggle
a difficult process

Balch reads telegrams in her room at the Newton-Wellesley Hospital.

barbed-wire
a fence with sharp metal points

criminals
lawbreakers

concerned
troubled

communities
neighborhoods

27

Vocabulary Skill Builder

■ Match each word with its meaning.

_____ 1. refugees

_____ 2. outspoken

_____ 3. concerned

_____ 4. communities

_____ 5. barbed-wire

_____ 6. conditions

_____ 7. criminals

a. worried

b. people who have broken the law

c. wire with sharp points

d. the state of things

e. neighborhoods

f. open and honest

g. people who have left their homes to escape danger

■ Write a paragraph using these three words from the story.

evil: very bad
painful: causing hurt
struggle: something demanding much effort

_____

_____

_____

_____

_____

_____

_____

_____

Read and Remember

■ Find the best ending for each sentence. Fill in the circle next to it.

1. Emily Balch lost her teaching position at Wellesley College because of her ideas about
   ○ a. the law.   ○ b. Jews.
   ○ c. war.

2. Balch helped dozens of German Jews find
   ○ a. jobs.   ○ b. new homes.
   ○ c. their children.

3. Balch believed that Hitler had to be
   ○ a. supported.   ○ b. stopped.
   ○ c. trained.

4. Balch believed that wars were
   ○ a. necessary.   ○ b. a terrible waste.
   ○ c. easy to win.

5. Balch won the Nobel Prize for the work she did
   ○ a. during World War II.   ○ b. throughout her life.
   ○ c. in 1942.

Think and Apply — Finding the Sequence

■ Number the sentences to show the order in which things happened in the story. The first one is done for you.

_____ Balch sent puzzles and school supplies to Japanese-American children.

_____ World War II began.

_____ Emily Balch was given a Nobel Peace Prize.

__1__ Balch lost her teaching job at Wellesley College.

_____ Hitler came to power in Germany.

Albert Luthuli

Leader and Hero

concrete
mixture of sand, clay, and water

*T*he old Zulu chief moved slowly up the dusty road in Groutville, South Africa. He was heading toward a small cottage at the end of the road. This was the chief's home. He had built it himself out of tin and **concrete** blocks.

As he walked, a car pulled up beside him. "I have a message for you," the driver called out. "You have just been awarded the most important prize in the world. You have won the Nobel Peace Prize!"

From Teacher to Chief

Chief Albert John Mvumbi Luthuli could not believe his ears. For years he had been fighting for the rights of black South Africans. During this time it had seemed that nobody else cared about him or his people. Now, in October of 1961, the world was taking notice.

"We have not had many **material triumphs**," he told a reporter, "but we have kept the spirit of freedom alive in ourselves and in others. Now comes the new **encouragement** of the Nobel Prize. We thank God and our brothers around the world for remembering us!"

Word of the award spread quickly. No black African had ever won a Nobel Prize before. In the past, the Peace Prize had usually gone to someone from Europe or America. But nobody **deserved** this award more than Chief Luthuli.

Luthuli had grown up in Groutville. He had gone to a school set up by white church workers. Here Luthuli came to believe that all people were important. All people should have the same **basic** rights. All should be able to live their lives with **dignity**.

material
measurable

triumphs
successes

encouragement
the giving of hope

deserved
was worthy of

basic
important

dignity
sense of self-worth

Luthuli visiting with Senator Robert F. Kennedy.

In 1921, when Luthuli was 23 years old, he became a teacher at Adams College. For fifteen years, he taught Zulu music and the Zulu language. During this time, he married and had seven children. In 1933, Luthuli was approached by men from his home village. They were the leaders of Groutville's Zulu tribe. They wanted him to be their chief. "No," he told them, "I am a teacher, not a chief." Again the leaders came to him. And again he turned them down.

At last, in 1936, Luthuli changed his mind. He knew his people didn't have much money or farmland. They needed a strong leader.

Luthuli in the Nobel Institute in Oslo, looking at portraits of former Nobel Peace Prize Winners.

Stirring Up Hope

Leaving Adams College proved to be a turning point in Luthuli's life. As Zulu chief, he took a close look at the way his people were being treated. Blacks made up 80% of the people in South Africa. Yet whites controlled the country. Whites owned almost all the good land. Whites decided where blacks could live, work, and travel. Luthuli knew this was wrong. He wanted to work to change these things.

In 1945, Luthuli joined the African National Congress (ANC). This group was trying to improve life for black South Africans. It was trying to get all black tribes to join together to fight the unfair laws. Over time, Luthuli became a leader of the ANC. In 1952, he helped lead a **protest** against the laws. The protest was not bloody. Blacks did not hurt anybody. They broke many laws, but they did so quietly and peacefully. They walked into libraries that were for "whites only." They sat on "whites only" benches. They entered cities where only whites lived. Police officers quickly **arrested** them. But each day other blacks repeated the actions. Soon the government had arrested 8,000 people.

protest
event where people speak or act out against something

arrested
held by the police

When police arrested Luthuli, they asked him to quit the ANC. He refused. Government officers told him they would no longer consider him a Zulu chief. But neither Luthuli nor his people cared. To black South Africans, Luthuli would always be "Chief." A month later, Luthuli became president of the ANC. He began traveling all over South Africa. Everywhere he went, he was cheered by crowds of blacks. "Today we have reached a stage where we have almost no rights at all," he told them. "We must work to change that. Our work must be done peacefully, but openly and boldly."

White leaders could see that Luthuli was stirring up hope among blacks. They said he could not visit any city for two years.

After the two years had passed, Luthuli headed out again. The crowds that came to see him were bigger than ever. White leaders stepped in with another two-year sentence. This time Luthuli had to stay in his village of Groutville.

A Leader, A Hero

By now Luthuli was 56 years old. He was not in good health. While in Groutville, he suffered a stroke. His wife had to beg police officers to take him to a hospital. At last, when they saw how sick he was, they let him go. He spent two months in the hospital before returning home.

In July of 1956, Luthuli was free to travel again. Blacks around the country were eager to see him. He was their leader, their hero. His words and actions set an example for all of them to follow. Luthuli was ready to do whatever he could to help them. But new troubles lay ahead. White leaders still wanted to get rid of him. In December of 1956, they arrested him. They said he was a danger to the country. For nine months, they kept him in jail with 155 other leaders.

A protest in South Africa

By now, Luthuli was the strongest black leader in South Africa. From prison he planned a new wave of protests. When Luthuli got out of jail, he continued working for black rights.

35,000 march through Capetown for peace and freedom.

In 1959, white leaders again ordered Luthuli back to his home village of Groutville. This time they told him he had to stay there for five years.

And so it was in Groutville that Luthuli learned of his Nobel Peace Prize. He was not allowed to leave the country to accept the award in person. But Luthuli was **overjoyed** with the honor. "The fight is not over," he thought to himself. "But at least now we are not alone. The world knows and cares about our struggle."

overjoyed
very happy

Vocabulary Skill Builder

Part A

■ Read each sentence. Fill in the circle next to the best meaning for the word in dark print. If you need help, use the Glossary.

1. Chief Luthuli lived in a small house made of **concrete** blocks.
   ○ a. sand and clay mixture   ○ b. smooth   ○ c. burned wood

2. At first, black South Africans had few **material** successes.
   ○ a. measurable   ○ b. belonging to mothers   ○ c. peaceful

3. Luthuli hoped his Nobel Prize would lead to **triumphs** for blacks.
   ○ a. difficult times   ○ b. jobs   ○ c. successes

4. Nobody **deserved** the Nobel Peace Prize more than Luthuli.
   ○ a. planned   ○ b. had earned   ○ c. cared about

5. Luthuli thought all people should be able to live with **dignity**.
   ○ a. honor   ○ b. plenty to eat   ○ c. adventure

Part B

■ Write the best word to complete each sentence. Use each word once.

| encouragement | basic | protests |
| arrested | overjoyed | |

Chief Luthuli worked hard to win (1)_____ rights for black

South Africans. He gave many speeches and helped organize

(2)_____ . Several times he was (3)_____ .

When he won the Nobel Peace Prize in 1961, he was

(4)_____ . He felt the prize would give black South

Africans (5)_____ to keep fighting for their rights.

Read and Remember

■ Some of the statements below are true. Others are false. Place a check in front of the three things that Chief Luthuli did.

_____ 1. Albert Luthuli became a Zulu chief.

_____ 2. Chief Luthuli set fire to "white" libraries.

_____ 3. Chief Luthuli created the African National Congress.

_____ 4. Chief Luthuli traveled around South Africa encouraging blacks to fight for their rights.

_____ 5. Chief Luthuli spent nine months in jail.

_____ 6. Chief Luthuli ordered blacks to stay in their home villages.

Write Your Ideas

■ Pretend you are Albert Luthuli. You just learned that you have won the Nobel Peace Prize. Write a letter to one of your children expressing your thoughts and feelings.

Dear _____ ,

_____

_____

_____

_____

_____

_____

_____

_____

_____

_____

Nelly Sachs

A Voice for Her People

visas
papers allowing
travel in another
country

novel
book

Nelly Sachs sat next to her sick mother. "What happens if we don't get the **visas**?" her mother asked in a trembling voice. Nelly didn't say anything. Her mother knew the answer.

In 1940, all German Jews knew the answer. One by one, Jews were disappearing. Nazi soldiers were sending them to death camps.

Forced Out

Nelly Sachs was an only child born in Germany in 1891. She was a shy Jewish girl. At age fifteen, Nelly read a story by Selma Lagerlöf. As things turned out, reading this **novel** probably saved her life.

Lagerlöf was a famous Swedish writer. Her novel greatly impressed Nelly. Nelly wrote Lagerlöf a letter. Lagerlöf wrote back. For the next 35 years, the two women exchanged letters.

During these years, there were many changes in Nelly's life. In 1930, her father died. Then in 1933, Hitler came to power in Germany. Hitler made it clear that he hated Jews. When World War II started in 1939, Hitler began sending huge numbers of Jews to death camps.

Once the war began, Nelly and her mother stayed out of sight. Everyday, more of their friends disappeared. By 1940, Nelly knew she could hide no longer. She had learned that she would soon be sent to a forced **labor** camp.

labor
work

Selma Lagerlöf in her library

Once again Nelly wrote to Selma Lagerlöf. "Perhaps she can help us get out of Germany," Nelly said to her mother. As the Sachs waited nervously, Lagerlöf went to the Swedish royal family. She asked for visas that would allow the Sachs to move to Sweden. When Nelly heard that the visas had been granted, she cried tears of joy.

Living and Writing in Sweden

But before Nelly and her mother got to Sweden, Lagerlöf died. They were alone in a **foreign** land. They had little money. Nelly worked hard to learn Swedish. She earned some money by **translating** Swedish poems into German.

By the time World War II ended, six million Jews had been killed. People around the world were **horrified** when they learned about the death camps. Many were very **bitter**. At first Nelly felt this way, too. She began writing poems about what had happened to her people. "I only wrote because I had to free myself," she later said.

A Voice for Her People

After Hitler, some people said that poems could never again be written in German. How could poetry be written in a language that had been used to sentence so many people to death?

Over the next twenty years, Nelly proved these people wrong. She wrote German poems and plays about the death camps. Her works captured the suffering of the Jewish people. Her poems used images of dust and smoke to show death. Butterflies **represented** the human spirit.

In 1966, Nelly Sachs shared the Nobel Prize for **Literature** with Shmuel Yosef Agnon. Agnon wrote poems about Israel. Israel is the Jewish state that was set up after World War II. When giving out the Nobel Prizes, someone said the two writers "represent Israel's message to our time."

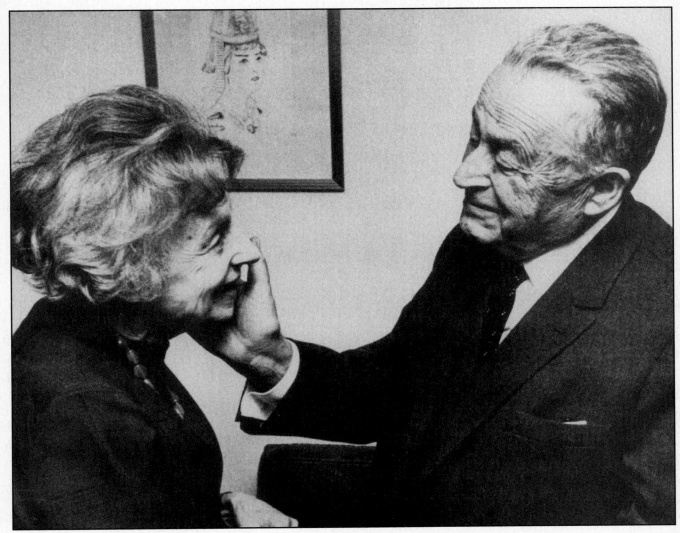

Nelly Sachs and Yosef Agnon meet for the first time to receive their awards in Sweden.

For a moment, Nelly stopped smiling. She felt that her words were for all Jews, not just the people of Israel. When it was her time to speak, she stood up and said, "Agnon represents the State of Israel. I represent the **tragedy** of the Jewish people."

tragedy
very sad event

Vocabulary Skill Builder

■ Complete the following sentences by writing the missing words in the spaces. Choose from the words in the box. When you are finished, the letters in the boxes will describe Nelly Sachs.

novel	foreign	visas	translating	horrified
labor	bitter	tragedy	represented	literature

1. Nelly and her mother could not leave Germany without _____ .

___ ___ ___ ☐ ___

2. To Nelly and her mother, Sweden was a place that was _____ .

___ ___ ___ ___ ___ ☐ ___

3. People who knew about the death camps were _____ .

___ ___ ___ ☐ ___ ___ ___ ___ .

4. Nelly won the Nobel Prize for _____ .

___ ___ ___ ☐ ___ ___ ___ ___ ___

5. World War II was a _____ .

___ ___ ☐ ___ ___ ___ ___

6. After the war, many people felt _____ .

___ ___ ___ ☐ ___ ___

7. In Nelly's poems, the human spirit was what butterflies _____ .

___ ___ ☐ ___ ___ ___ ___ ___ ___ ___

8. At some Nazi camps, Jews were forced to do _____ .

___ ___ ___ ☐ ___

9. Nelly loved reading Selma Lagerlöf's _____ .

___ ___ ___ ☐ ___ ___

10. In Sweden, Nelly made money by _____ .

___ ___ ___ ___ ___ ___ ___ ☐ ___ ___ ___

Read and Remember

■ Answer the questions.

1. What happened to millions of German Jews during World War II?

_____

_____

2. How did Selma Lagerlöf help Nelly Sachs and her mother? _____

_____

_____

3. What were Nelly's poems about? _____

4. In Nelly's poems, what images stand for death? _____

_____

5. Why did Nelly say she did not represent the state of Israel? _____

_____

_____

Think and Apply — Cause and Effect

■ Complete the following sentences.

1. Nelly Sachs began writing to Selma Lagerlöf because _____

_____

2. Nelly Sachs wanted to leave Germany because _____

_____

3. After World War II, some people thought poems would never again be written in German because _____

_____

4. Nelly began writing poems because _____

_____

Alexander Solzhenitsyn

A Voice for Freedom

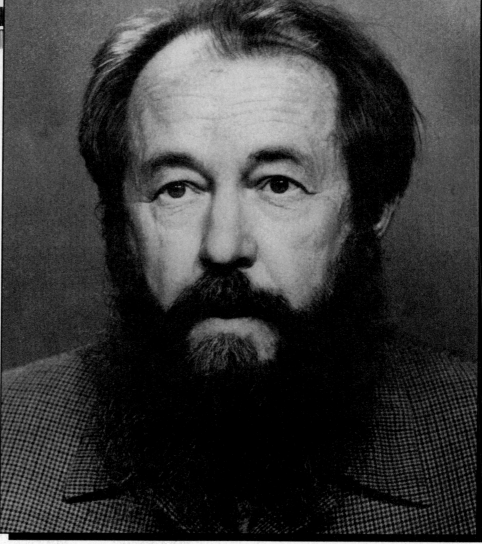

cot
narrow bed

$\mathbb{A}$lexander Solzhenitsyn closed his eyes. He tried to forget he was lying on a hard army **cot** in a cold tent far from home.

At last he drifted off to sleep. Suddenly, someone shined a bright light in his face. Solzhenitsyn opened his eyes. Standing over him were several members of the secret police. "Captain Alexander Solzhenitsyn?" one of them said in a rough voice. "You must come with us. You are under arrest."

From Hero to Prisoner

Solzhenitsyn's heart froze when he saw the secret police. In 1945, everyone in the Soviet Union feared the secret police. These men worked directly for Soviet leader Joseph Stalin. If someone **criticized** Stalin, the secret police would arrest the person. He or she would be dragged off to prison or a labor camp.

Before World War II started, Solzhenitsyn had lived a simple life as a math teacher. He had joined the army in 1941. He had risen to the rank of captain. He had fought on the front lines and had been wounded several times. Twice he had won medals for bravery. "Why are you arresting me?" Solzhenitsyn cried as he was led away. The secret police did not answer.

Solzhenitsyn gathering information for a book

Only later did Solzhenitsyn find out why he had been arrested. A few months earlier, he had written a letter to a friend. In the letter, Solzhenitsyn **referred** to Stalin. The Soviet leader was a cruel man who had killed millions of people. He had put

45

millions more in prison. In his letter, Solzhenitsyn made fun of Stalin. He called him "the whiskered one" and a "busybody."

The secret police opened and read the letter. They saw that Solzhenitsyn was writing about their leader. And so in February of 1945, they arrested him.

After his arrest, Solzhenitsyn lost the title of captain. He was questioned and beaten. Then he was sentenced to eight years in prison.

Solzhenitsyn spent time in three different prisons. He lived through many terrible days. He became very ill. At one point prison guards thought he would die.

At last though, Solzhenitsyn was lucky. He was sent to Marfino, a prison where scientists and **mathematicians** did research. Conditions were better there than in other prisons. Solzhenitsyn said, "My training in mathematics saved my life."

mathematicians people who work with numbers

A Brief Moment of Freedom

In 1956, Solzhenitsyn finally became a free man again. He moved to the city of Ryazan, southeast of Moscow. By that time Joseph Stalin had died. A new leader named Nikita Khrushchev had taken over. Khrushchev didn't like Stalin. He wanted to show what a bad leader Stalin had been. He began criticizing Stalin. He allowed others to do the same.

Solzhenitsyn was working as a high school teacher. But he also made time to write. By 1962, he had finished a book. He called it *One Day in the Life of Ivan Denisovich*. It told the sad story of one day in the life of a prisoner during Stalin's rule. Much of it was based on Solzhenitsyn's personal experience.

Solzhenitsyn sent his story to a magazine editor. The editor's name was Alexander Tvardovsky. Tvardovsky liked to look over new stories before going to sleep. Lying in bed, he glanced at each one before tossing it aside. When he picked up

Solzhenitsyn giving a speech

One Day in the Life of Ivan Denisovich, he read the first ten lines. Tvardovsky later said, "Suddenly I felt that I couldn't read it like this. I had to do something more **appropriate**. So I got up. I put on my best black suit, a white shirt, a tie, and my good shoes. Then I sat at my desk and read a new **classic**."

appropriate
fitting

classic
fine book

The next day, Tvardovsky sent the novel to Khrushchev. The Soviet leader loved it. Khrushchev ordered 100,000 copies printed. They sold out in a few days. The book passed from one person to another. Before long, millions of people had read the book.

More Troubles

In 1964, the brief moment of freedom in the Soviet Union ended. Khrushchev was removed from power. The new Soviet leader said good things about Stalin. Stalin's picture appeared on television for the first time in nine years. Slowly, copies of *One Day in the Life of Ivan Denisovich* became harder to find.

Solzhenitsyn's home in Vermont

Solzhenitsyn kept writing. But he found it difficult to get his books printed. On May 16, 1967, he wrote an open letter to other Soviet writers. He complained that he was not allowed to write what he wanted. He said that the secret police were stealing his papers. He also said that many writers had been sent to prison. He wrote, "No one can block the road to the truth. In order to **advance** it, I am willing to accept even **death**."

advance
help the progress of

death
the end of life

This bold letter put Solzhenitsyn in real danger. Soviet leaders attacked him. They said his books helped the enemies of the Soviet Union. They **banned** his writings. Still, copies of his new novels were being sneaked out of the Soviet Union. They were printed in other countries.

People around the world cheered Solzhenitsyn. They saw him as a champion of truth and freedom. In 1970, he won the Nobel Prize for Literature. But Soviet leaders would not let him go to Norway to receive the prize.

In 1974, Solzhenitsyn was arrested and charged with **treason**. He was kicked out of the Soviet Union. In time, he settled in a small town in Vermont. There, at last, Solzhenitsyn could write whatever he wanted.

banned
made something against the law

treason
helping the enemies of one's country

Alexander and Natalie Solzhenitsyn during a Fourth of July celebration.

Vocabulary Skill Builder

■ Match each word with its meaning.

____ 1. appropriate   a. said bad things about

____ 2. treason   b. proper and fitting

____ 3. advance   c. narrow bed

____ 4. criticized   d. people who work with math

____ 5. death   e. helping your country's enemies

____ 6. mathematicians   f. helping the progress of something

____ 7. cot   g. end of life

■ Write a paragraph using these three words from the story.

referred: directed attention to
banned: made something against the law
classic: a fine book or piece of art

_____

_____

_____

_____

_____

_____

_____

_____

Read and Remember

■ Find the best ending for each sentence. Fill in the circle next to it.

1. During World War II, Solzhenitsyn showed that he was
   ○ a. frightened of guns.   ○ b. good with numbers.   ○ c. brave.

2. Solzhenitsyn first got in trouble with the secret police by writing a
   ○ a. letter.   ○ b. speech.   ○ c. book.

3. Solzhenitsyn did not like
   ○ a. to write.   ○ b. Joseph Stalin.   ○ c. Alexander Tvardovsky.

4. The importance of Solzhenitsyn's story *One Day in the Life of Ivan Denisovich* was noticed by
   ○ a. a magazine editor.   ○ b. no one.   ○ c. Stalin.

5. Four years after Solzhenitsyn won the Nobel Prize, Soviet leaders forced him to
   ○ a. go to prison.   ○ b. leave the country.   ○ c. burn his books.

Write Your Ideas

■ Pretend you are Alexander Solzhenitsyn. Write a letter to a friend back home describing what it is like to live in the United States.

Dear _____ ,

_____

_____

_____

_____

_____

_____

_____

_____

Betty Williams and Mairead Corrigan

The Founding of Peace People

getaway
escape

*T*he driver of the IRA **getaway** car stepped on the gas. For a moment, it looked as though he would escape. But the British soldiers who were chasing him managed to fire a few shots. One of the bullets killed the driver, and the car spun wildly out of control. People screamed as the car jumped the curb. It ran into Anne Maguire and her three young children. Maguire was badly hurt. Her children were all killed.

800 Years of Fighting

The accident took place in West Belfast, Northern Ireland, on August 10, 1976. People all over the city were saddened by the children's deaths. But **violence** like this happened all the time. It was part of life in Northern Ireland. As long as Catholics

violence
harmful action

and Protestants were fighting for control of the area, **innocent** people would be killed. "It's been going on for years," the people said. "There is nothing we can do."

For 800 years Catholics and Protestants had been fighting about who should control Northern Ireland. The Irish Republican Army (IRA) wanted Northern Ireland to be Catholic. They wanted it to belong to the Catholic country of Ireland. British soldiers and the Ulster Defense Association (UDA) wanted Northern Ireland to be Protestant. They wanted it to stay part of the United Kingdom.

innocent
doing no wrong

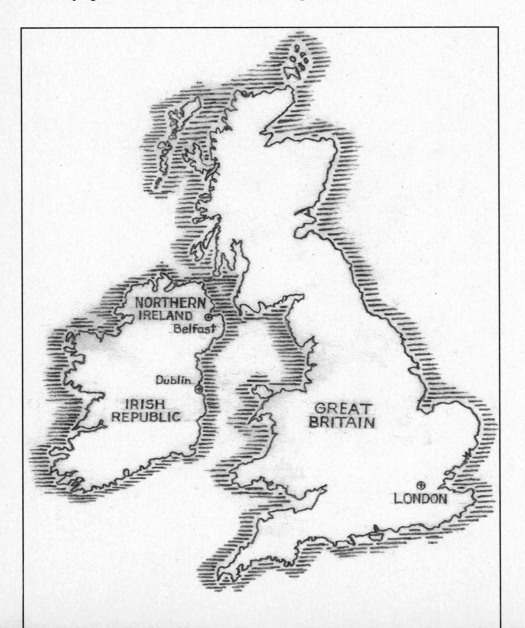

Map of Ireland and Great Britain

Both sides used violence. The IRA staged **terrorist** attacks to frighten Protestants. British soldiers and UDA members fought back by **targeting** IRA homes and offices. Neither side would give up. Year after year, the violence continued. Sometimes the bullets hit their mark. But all too often, innocent people suffered. The deaths of Anne Maguire's children were the latest examples of this. British soldiers had meant to kill the driver of the IRA getaway car. To them it was simply bad luck that the children had also been killed.

Speaking Out Against the Violence

For some people, however, the deaths of the Maguire children were more than just "bad luck." For Anne Maguire's sister, Mairead Corrigan, they were a turning point. She promised herself that the deaths would not be forgotten–that they would have meaning. Corrigan decided to do what no other Catholic had dared to do. She decided to speak out openly against the IRA and their terrorist attacks.

"You are crazy," her neighbors told her. "The IRA will kill you. They kill anyone who gets in their way. And you–you are Catholic! To them you will be a **traitor**!"

But Corrigan didn't care. She appeared on television. Her voice shook as she told how her family was suffering. She called for the IRA to stop all terrorist attacks.

In another home in West Belfast, a woman named Betty Williams was having the same thoughts. Williams was a Catholic woman with two small children of her own. She lived near the scene of the accident. She had seen it happen. Earlier, Williams had supported the IRA. She wanted

Catholics in Northern Ireland to have more rights. But the violence was too much for her.

"The price is too high," she thought. Angrily she remembered all the lives ruined by violence. "Our kids are being raised in a war **zone**. They don't know how to play–give them a book and they draw tanks and guns on it. Now three more innocent children have been killed!"

zone
area

Williams and Corrigan show telegrams of support they have received.

declaring
stating strongly

Within hours of the accident, Williams came up with a plan. "I am **declaring** war on war," she said. She drew up a statement calling for an end to the fighting. She went door to door asking women to sign it. When Mairead Corrigan heard about it, she gave Williams a call. Together the two women planned a march for peace.

Williams and Corrigan receiving the Nobel Peace Prize

supporters
people who believe
in a cause

On August 14, 10,000 women answered the call. They poured into the streets, praying and singing songs. Together they walked to the spot where the Maguire children were buried. IRA **supporters** tried to block their path, but the women pushed through.

Say Peace! Think Peace!

The next day Corrigan and Williams founded the Community of Peace People. With a reporter named Ciaran McKeown, they planned weekly marches in Ireland and the United Kingdom. Some **observers** didn't think the marches would work.

But Corrigan and Williams believed that ordinary women–wives, mothers, sisters–could make a difference. By the third march, Protestant and Catholic women were marching arm in arm. Soon men also joined the movement.

But new problems arose. Both the IRA and the UDA threatened the women. Stones were thrown at them as they marched. Once Williams was even attacked in her own home. Still, she and Corrigan kept marching. "Say peace! Think peace!" they called out in city after city. "Pray peace, dream for peace, walk with peace in your heart!"

To the surprise of some observers, the marches were a huge success. Often as many as 20,000 people turned out for them. The Community of Peace People did not end the violence. But they helped people believe that peace was possible. By the end of 1977, the number of killings had been cut in half. "There is still a long way to go," Corrigan and Williams said. "But more and more people are listening to our message."

Certainly the rest of the world was listening. In 1977, Corrigan and Williams were given the Nobel Peace Prize for trying to bring peace to war-torn Northern Ireland.

observers
people who watch

57

Vocabulary Skill Builder

■ Use the clues to complete the puzzle. Choose from the words in the box.

getaway
violence
innocent
terrorist
targeting
traitor
zone
declaring
supporters
observers

Across

2. person who tries to hurt others in surprise attacks

3. escape

4. people who believe in a cause

8. harmful force

9. stating strongly

Down

1. person who does something to hurt his or her country

2. aiming at

5. those who watch

6. having done nothing wrong

7. area

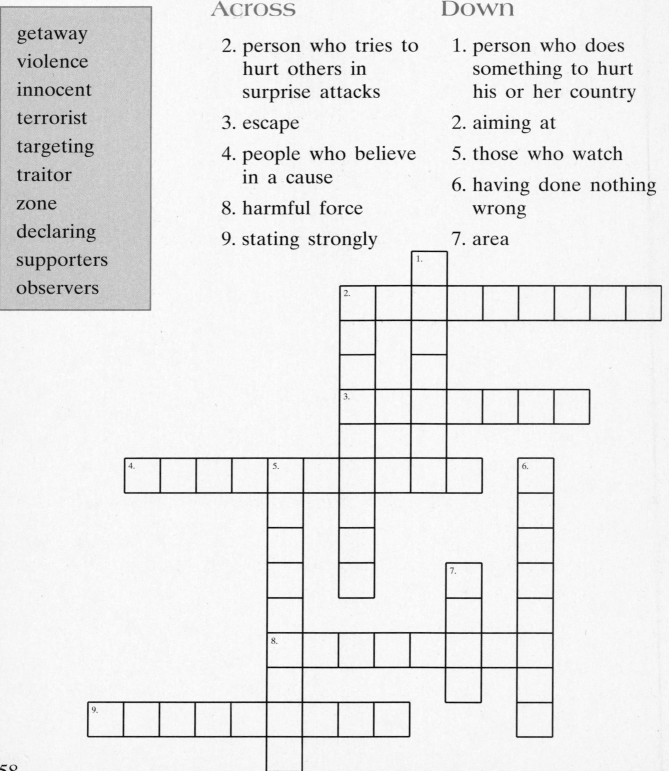

Read and Remember

■ Some of the statements below are true. Others are false. Place a check in front of the three things that happened in the story.

_____ 1. Anne Maguire was the driver of an IRA getaway car.

_____ 2. Betty Williams and Mairead Corrigan planned weekly marches in Ireland and the United Kingdom.

_____ 3. Protestants and Catholics joined the Community of Peace People.

_____ 4. The Irish Republican Army (IRA) worked to keep Northern Ireland part of the United Kingdom.

_____ 5. British soldiers were pleased that Mairead Corrigan's sister had been killed.

_____ 6. Ten thousand women marched to the spot where the Maguire children were buried.

Think and Apply — Main Ideas

■ Underline the two most important ideas from the story.

1. Betty Williams and Mairead Corrigan tried to end the fighting between Catholics and Protestants.

2. Betty Williams and Mairead Corrigan worked with a reporter named Ciaran McKeown.

3. Betty Williams and Mairead Corrigan began working together after Anne Maguire's children were killed.

4. Betty Williams and Mairead Corrigan's "Community of Peace People" helped people believe that peace was possible.

5. Betty Williams and Mairead Corrigan made enemies within both the UDA and the IRA.

Gabriel García Márquez

Gifted Storyteller

gloomy
sad

The boy stared out the library window. The sky was turning grey. He could see storm clouds gathering in the distance. Soon, he knew, it would be raining. To fourteen-year-old Gabriel García Márquez, the world seemed dark and **gloomy**.

"You're not from around here, are you?" asked the kind old woman who ran the library.

Gabriel shook his head. He was new to Zipaquirá, Columbia. This city was his home now. But to him it seemed like the saddest place in the world.

Life in Aracataca

Gabriel García Márquez was the oldest of sixteen children. He was born in 1928 in a tiny town near the Caribbean Sea. Aracataca was a **tropical** village in Columbia. Gabriel's parents were young. They wanted to leave Aracataca. They wanted to go to another village where they could find better jobs. They did not, however, want to take their baby son with them. Instead, they left him with his grandparents.

Gabriel García Márquez stayed with his grandparents for eight years. He grew up listening to the stories of these two wonderful, **eccentric** old people. Gabriel's grandfather loved to take him places and tell him stories about Columbia's history. Gabriel's grandmother also told stories. Her tales, however, were of a different kind.

tropical
warm all-year long

eccentric
different or odd

García Márquez spent his early years in a village on the coast.

Gabriel's grandmother told stories about wild things. She talked about strange people with amazing powers. She enjoyed telling Gabriel about this make-believe world. She was a great storyteller. She could make even the wildest story seem true. Young Gabriel loved listening to her. But he was also frightened. As he later said, "My grandmother was a **superstitious** woman with a **vivid** imagination who terrified me, night after night, with her stories . . . ."

Márquez receives the literature award from King Carl Gustaf.

A Lonely Life

Gabriel liked living with his grandparents. But in many ways it was a lonely life. He spent much of his time wandering around his grandparents' big house all by himself. He soon learned what **solitude** means. It means being alone.

In 1936, Gabriel's grandfather died. By this time his grandmother was blind. She could no longer take care of Gabriel. Sadly, she sent him off to live with his parents. In 1942, Gabriel went even farther away. He was sent to Zipaquirá to finish high school.

In the Style of His Grandmother

In Zipaquirá, Gabriel had to deal with a new kind of loneliness. He was no longer near any of his family. He was six hundred miles from the warm beaches of Aracataca. Zipaquirá was a cold, rainy city high in the mountains. Gabriel's school was dark and damp. To escape from this gloomy new world, Gabriel turned to books. He read and read. He spent every Sunday in the library.

The more Gabriel read, the more interested he became in writing. He finished school and left Zipaquirá in 1946. He became a **journalist**. In his free time, he wrote short stories. He found himself using a familiar **style**. "It's the style of my grandmother!" he thought to himself. "It's the style she used when she told stories."

This style helped Gabriel García Márquez become a famous writer. In 1982, he won the Nobel Prize for Literature. Gabriel García Márquez found that **memories** from his early years helped him in other ways, as well. Many of his stories were set in tropical towns very much like Aracataca. They were filled with **imaginary** events. And almost all of his writings dealt with solitude. One of his most famous books was called *One Hundred Years of Solitude*.

Márquez's book *One Hundred Years of Solitude*

solitude
being alone

journalist
writer for a newspaper

style
manner of doing something

memories
things remembered from the past

imaginary
not real

Vocabulary Skill Builder

■ Complete the following sentences by writing the missing words in the spaces. Choose from the words in the box. When you are finished, the letters in the boxes will tell you what Gabriel García Márquez is famous for.

gloomy	tropical	eccentric	style	journalist
imaginary	memories	solitude	vivid	superstitious

1. Gabriel thought Zipaquirá was _____ .

⬚ _ □ _ _ _ _

2. His grandmother's imagination was _____ .

□ _ □ _ _ _

3. Gabriel's grandmother was very _____ .

_ _ _ _ _ _ □ _ _ _ _ _ _

4. As a child, García Márquez learned the meaning of _____ .

_ _ _ _ _ _ _ □

5. Gabriel's grandparents were quite _____ .

_ _ _ _ _ _ _ □ _

6. Most events in García Márquez's books are _____ .

_ _ _ _ _ _ □ _ _

7 When writing stories, Gabriel used his grandmother's _____ .

□ _ _ _ _ _

8. After finishing school, García Márquez became a _____ .

_ _ □ _ _ _ _ _ _ _

9. The weather in Aracataca could be described as _____ .

_ □ _ _ _ _ _ _

10. García Márquez's stories included his childhood _____ .

_ □ _ _ _ _ _ _

Read and Remember

■ Answer the questions.

1. Why did Gabriel García Márquez live with his grandparents for the first eight years of his life? _____

_____

2. How did young Gabriel feel about the stories his grandmother told him? _____

_____

3. Why didn't Gabriel García Márquez like the city of Zipaquirá?

_____

_____

4. Why did Gabriel spend so much of his time in Zipaquirá reading?

_____

_____

5. What are García Márquez's books like? _____

_____

Write Your Ideas

■ Write three important facts you learned about Gabriel García Márquez.

1. _____

_____

2. _____

_____

3. _____

_____

Barbara McClintock

Ahead of Her Times

*I*t was the summer of 1919. For weeks, Barbara McClintock had been begging her parents to let her go to college. They always said no. But one day, they had a change of heart.

"As you know, your father and I think college is for men," Mrs. McClintock said. "It's no place for a seventeen-year-old girl. But we want you to be happy. So if you really want to . . . you can go." Barbara hugged her parents with joy.

Indian Corn

In the fall of 1919, Barbara McClintock entered Cornell University. She began studying **genetics**. Genetics is the study of how plants and animals pass **traits** to their **offspring**. Genetics explains

genetics
study of how features are passed from parents to their children

traits
features

offspring
children; young ones

how brown-eyed parents can have a blue-eyed child. It explains how traits such as height and hair color are passed from one **generation** to the next.

McClintock loved genetics. Insects and plants were used to study how traits were passed. Indian corn was often studied because its **kernels** and leaves varied greatly in color.

McClintock became a professor and then a **researcher**. She spent the next 50 years studying Indian corn. It became her life's work. She spent many hours each day growing Indian corn and studying the color changes from one generation to the next.

generation
grandparent, parent, child, etc.

kernels
seeds

researcher
person who studies one subject

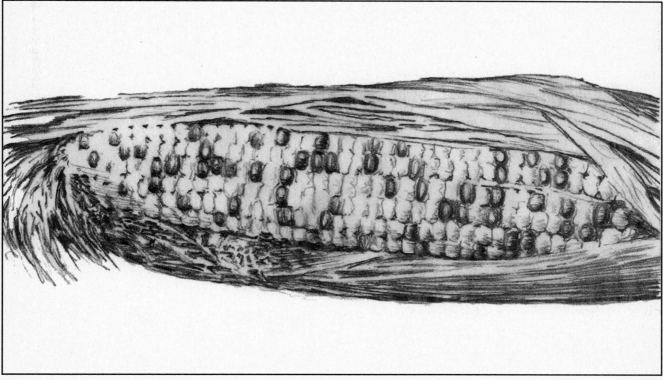
Indian corn

A New Discovery

One day in 1944, McClintock was working with two Indian corn plants. The plants were twins. They came from the same parent plants. Yet

McClintock holds ear of corn after being awarded the Nobel Prize for Medicine.

the twin plants did not look the same. The leaves of one plant had bright stripes. The leaves of the other had only faint stripes. Kernels from the two plants were also different.

"This isn't supposed to happen," McClintock thought. It took her six years to figure out what had happened. She checked and double-checked the corn. At last, in 1951, she wrote a paper telling the world about her discovery.

At that time, scientists believed that **genes**, the **units** that determine the passing on of traits, were always stationary. McClintock **challenged** that idea. She wrote that some genes jumped around. These "jumping genes" kept some information from being passed on to the next generation.

Ahead of Her Time

McClintock's paper offered an exciting new idea. Unfortunately, no one listened to her. Perhaps scientists refused to listen because she was a woman. More likely, they just didn't understand her work.

McClintock later said, "Other scientists thought I was crazy. **Absolutely** mad."

For a while she didn't care. But finally, she gave up writing about Indian corn. She said, "Nobody was reading me, so what was the use?"

At last, in the late 1960's, people started to believe McClintock. Other scientists studied her work. They found that she had been right all along.

McClintock wasn't surprised. She said, "When you know you're right, you don't care what others think. You know sooner or later it will come out in the wash."

In 1983, Barbara McClintock won the Nobel Prize. The money and fame meant little to her. But she did gain one important thing.

"The only thing I ever wanted," she said, "was the respect of other scientists. Now, I have it."

genes
bits of matter that carry qualities from parents to their young

units
things

challenged
questioned

Absolutely
completely

McClintock speaks during a press conference.

Vocabulary Skill Builder

Part A

■ Write the best word to complete each sentence. Use each word once.

challenged	genes	researcher
generation	genetics	

Barbara McClintock spent years working as a (1)_____ .

Her field of study was (2)_____ . McClintock wanted

to learn how certain qualities were passed from one

(3)_____ to the next. After careful study, she

(4)_____ the old ideas about this. In 1951, she wrote

a paper about "jumping (5)_____ ."

Part B

■ Read each sentence. Fill in the circle next to the best meaning for the word in dark print.

1. McClintock studied how plants pass **traits** to their young.
   ○ a. sicknesses   ○ b. certain features   ○ c. food

2. The **offspring** of brown-eyed people can have blue eyes.
   ○ a. parents   ○ b. cousins   ○ c. children

3. Different **kernels** of Indian corn vary greatly in color.
   ○ a. seeds   ○ b. leaves   ○ c. brands

4. "Jumping genes" were the **units** that caused plants to look different.
   ○ a. photographs   ○ b. mixture
   ○ c. single things within a larger whole

5. Other scientists thought McClintock was **absolutely** crazy.
   ○ a. completely   ○ b. secretly   ○ c. maybe

Read and Remember

■ Some of the statements below are true. Others are false. Place a check in front of the three things that Barbara McClintock did.

_____ 1. Barbara McClintock became a professor without ever going to college.

_____ 2. Barbara McClintock spent 50 years studying Indian corn.

_____ 3. Barbara McClintock married a genetics professor.

_____ 4. Barbara McClintock gave birth to twins who looked very different.

_____ 5. Barbara McClintock discovered "jumping genes."

_____ 6. Barbara McClintock finally earned the respect of other scientists.

Think and Apply—Finding the Sequence

■ Number the sentences to show the order in which things happened in the story. The first one is done for you.

1 _____ Barbara McClintock's parents agreed to let her go to Cornell University.

_____ Barbara McClintock wrote a paper telling the world about "jumping genes."

_____ Barbara McClintock noticed that twin corn plants did not have the same stripes on their leaves.

_____ Barbara McClintock stopped writing about Indian corn.

_____ Other scientists saw that McClintock's work made sense.

Wole Soyinka

The Man Who
Did Not Die

Wole Soyinka sat in a police office in Lagos, Nigeria. He felt worried. "I must be very careful," he thought. "If I say the wrong thing, Gowon will surely send me to prison."

At that moment, three guards burst into the room. They began wrapping heavy iron chains around Soyinka's feet. With a sinking feeling, Soyinka saw that it didn't matter what he said. Gowon, the president of Nigeria, had already decided. Wole Soyinka was going to jail.

The Life of a Prisoner

When Soyinka was chained and sent off to prison, many people were angry. After all, Wole Soyinka was a famous man. He was the most famous writer

in the African country of Nigeria. People in many
countries had read his plays and books. They knew
he was one of the best writers in the world. They
also knew that Soyinka was a good man. He hated
to see people suffer. It was his love of peace, in
fact, that got him in trouble with President Yakubu
Gowon.

The trouble started in the summer of 1967. A
group of Nigerians known as Ibos were getting
ready to fight the Nigerian government. Soyinka
didn't want a war. He wanted to help settle the
problem peacefully. To do this, he held a meeting
with the leaders of the Ibo group. That made
President Gowon angry. He **accused** Soyinka of
helping Ibo leaders plan the war. So, in August
of 1967, Wole Soyinka became a prisoner of the
Nigerian government.

accused
blamed

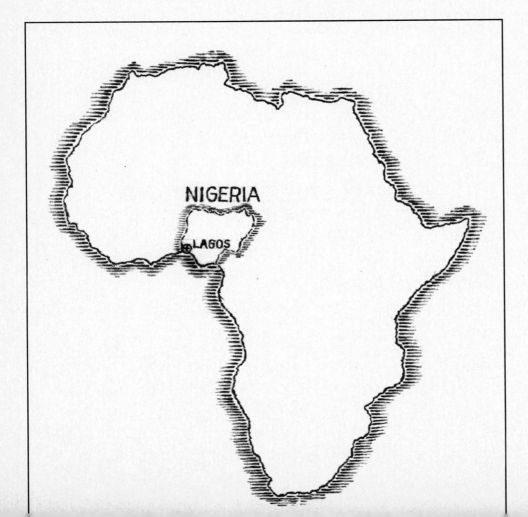

Map of Nigeria's
location in Africa.

For more than two years, Soyinka was kept in prison. No charges were brought against him. No one accused him of breaking any law. Still, the government refused to set him free.

Soyinka speaking to newsman

For the first four months, things were not too bad. Soyinka hated the government for holding him unfairly. But he soon adjusted to life in the prison. He read books from the prison library. He made up stories and told them to the other prisoners. He listened to guards talk about life beyond the prison walls. He even managed to **smuggle** some messages to the outside world.

smuggle
sneak

Soon, however, all that changed. Officials discovered that Soyinka was sending messages to friends outside the prison. These messages said bad things about President Gowon.

Gowon wanted to punish Soyinka and to cut him off from outside **contact**. Soyinka was moved to a different prison. He was put in a tiny unheated cell. This cell measured only four feet by eight feet. Everything in it was dark and dirty. There were only a few small windows set high up in the walls. Flies buzzed in the dusty air.

contact
being in touch with others

Soyinka was kept away from the other prisoners. Guards gave him nothing except his meals. He was allowed no books, no newspapers, no visitors. He had no contact at all with the outside world. He was not even allowed pen and paper for writing.

A Terrible Silence

The months that followed were bad ones for Soyinka. His only exercise came from walking around a small yard outside his cell. His hair grew long and tangled. As the cold winter winds swept in, his bare feet grew stiff and **numb**. His skin cracked. His eyes grew weak and watery. But for him, the worst part was the silence. He had no one to talk to and nothing to do. At times he felt he might go mad.

numb
having no feeling

Soyinka could think of only one way to keep from going crazy. He had to keep track of his thoughts. He had to write down his experiences so that someday he could share them with others.

Soyinka began looking around for a writing tool. At last he found one. A crow's feather floated into the yard outside his cell. Soyinka managed to pick it up without a guard seeing him. This feather

Soyinka in his office shortly after being awarded the Nobel Literature Prize

would be his pen! Toilet paper would serve as writing paper. With these things Soyinka could finally do what he so **desperately** needed to do. He could write!

Keeping His Spirit Alive

Soyinka suffered from loneliness and **despair** while he was in prison. He wrote,

> "All sounds now beat against the cell walls. I have begun to close in. I sit **motionless** . . . and wait."

Another time he wrote,

> "Days pass, weeks, months. Unnumbered days of sitting in the yard, staring into nothing . . ."

Soyinka used his feather pen to write poems and a play. Writing was his only comfort, the only thing that kept him **sane**.

After 27 months in prison, the Nigerian government finally set Wole Soyinka free. When Soyinka left the prison, his body was weak. But his mind was still strong. The long lonely months in prison had not broken his spirit. As a free man he continued to speak out against Gowon and others like him.

In 1972, Soyinka **published** the notes he had written in prison. He called this book *The Man Died*. Soyinka went on to write many other plays, books, and even songs. He also became an actor and professor of literature.

In 1986, Wole Soyinka was awarded the Nobel Prize for Literature. He was the first African ever to receive this prize. The prize was proof of his skill as a writer. It was also a **tribute** to his courage.

desperately
having great need

despair
loss of hope

motionless
not moving

sane
not crazy

published
printed and sold

tribute
something showing respect

Vocabulary Skill Builder

■ Use the clues to complete the puzzle. Choose from the words in the box.

tribute
motionless
sane
accused
despair
numb
desperately
contact
smuggle
published

Across

2. not moving
5. not crazy
6. having a great need
9. something showing respect
10. printed and sold

Down

1. being in touch with others
3. send secretly
4. loss of hope
7. blamed
8. having no feeling

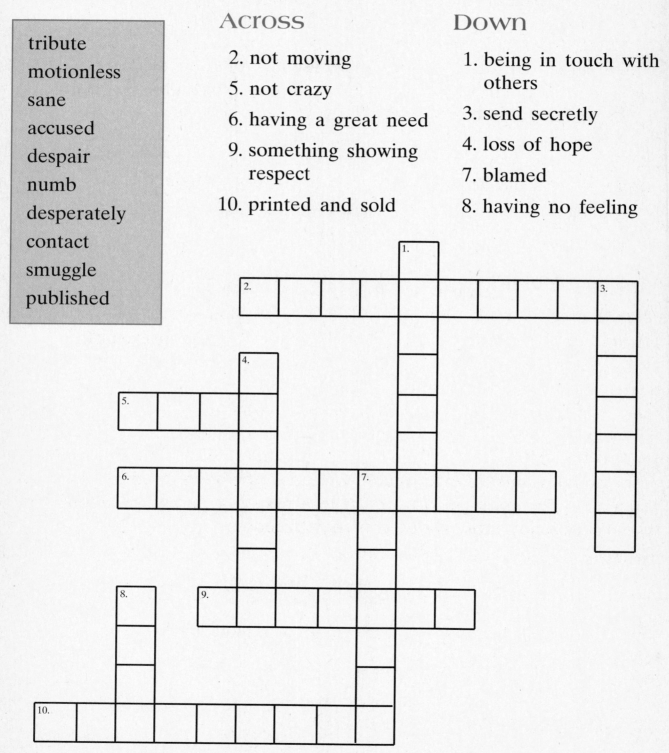

Read and Remember

■ Answer the questions.

1. Why did President Gowon put Wole Soyinka in jail? _____

_____

_____

2. Why were people upset when they heard that Wole Soyinka had been put in prison? _____

_____

3. In what ways did Soyinka suffer while he was in prison? _____

_____

_____

4. How was Soyinka able to write while in prison? _____

_____

5. What kinds of writing did Soyinka do while he was in prison? _____

_____

_____

Write Your Ideas

■ Pretend you are Wole Soyinka. You have just been freed after spending 27 months in prison. Write a poem or paragraph about what you enjoy most about your new freedom.

_____

_____

_____

_____

_____

_____

_____

Aung San Suu Kyi

The Struggle for Freedom

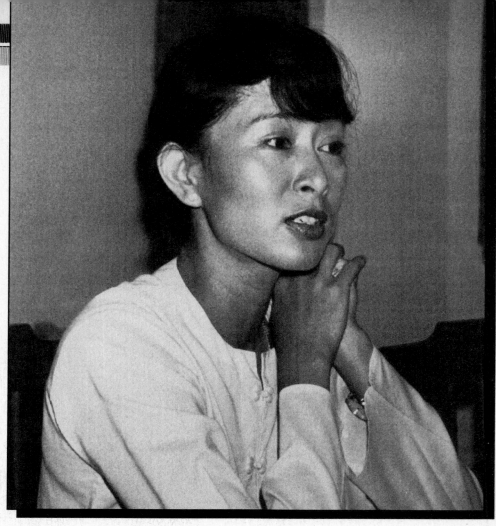

protesters
people who gather to speak or act out against something

brutal
very mean

military
army

*T*he **protesters** marched slowly down the street. Soldiers dropped to their knees and took aim. Their guns were pointed at Aung San Suu Kyi. They had orders to shoot her. Suu Kyi had spoken out against the **brutal military** leaders of her country. She was leading the movement against them.

At the last minute, the leaders had second thoughts. They ordered the soldiers to hold their fire. For the moment, Suu Kyi was safe.

Father and Daughter

When Suu Kyi was born in 1945, the South Asian country of Myanmar was called Burma. The people were struggling to win freedom from British rule.

Their leader, Aung San, was Suu Kyi's father. Sadly, in 1947, her father was shot and killed. The next year Burma gained its freedom.

After Suu Kyi grew up, she moved to Britain. She married a professor and had two sons. In April of 1988, she returned to Burma to care for her dying mother. Suu Kyi found her country in **turmoil**. Military leaders had taken over. People who dared to protest against the army were shot down in the streets.

turmoil
great confusion

Suu Kyi speaks to several thousand supporters in Ragoon.

Carrying on Her Father's Work

"I've got to do something to help," Suu Kyi thought. Within a few months, she had joined the protest movement. She gave speeches that **expressed** what many people were thinking. She said, "The people of Burma really want freedom. But first of all they want freedom from fear."

expressed
put into words

elections
voting for leaders

Democracy
government run by
the people

influence
power over people

Finally, the military leaders agreed to hold **elections** in May of 1990. By this time, Suu Kyi was the leader of the National League of **Democracy**. Myanmar's leaders feared her **influence**. In July of 1989, they placed her under house arrest.

They guarded her 24 hours a day. They cut her telephone lines. No one—not even her family—could visit her. Trapped inside her house, Suu Kyi read, played the piano, and prayed for her people.

Refusing to Give Up

Although Suu Kyi was out of sight, the Burmese people did not forget her. In the May election, they voted for her party. The National League of Democracy won 392 of the 485 seats. The military leaders were angry. They had been sure they would win. They refused to accept the election results. They arrested many people who had won seats.

Monks check election returns.

Stories about Suu Kyi spread to other countries. People everywhere wanted to see her freed. Myanmar's military leaders just wanted the problem to go away. They even gave Suu Kyi a chance to leave the country.

Billboard tells about her cause.

"I will go," she said, "but only if you do four things. You must honor the election results. You must free all innocent people you are holding in jail. You must let me give a speech on TV. And you must allow me to walk to the airport with my supporters."

The military leaders refused to do this. So Aung San Suu Kyi remained a prisoner in her own home. It was here that she learned that she had won the 1991 Nobel Peace Prize. She was **praised** for her "**nonviolent** struggle for democracy and human rights."

praised
spoken highly of

nonviolent
peaceful

83

Vocabulary Skill Builder

Part A

■ Write a paragraph using these three words from the story.

brutal: very mean
turmoil: great confusion
nonviolent: peaceful

_____

_____

_____

_____

_____

_____

_____

Part B

■ Find the best ending for each sentence. Fill in the circle next to it.

1. The **protesters** marched slowly down the street.
   ○ a. people who protect others   ○ b. people who shoot guns
   ○ c. people who speak out against something

2. Suu Kyi spoke out against the **military** leaders.
   ○ a. small number of   ○ b. army   ○ c. angry

3. Her speeches **expressed** what many people were thinking.
   ○ a. covered up   ○ b. put into words   ○ c. made simple

4. The leaders agreed to hold **elections**.
   ○ a. voting for leaders   ○ b. holidays   ○ c. special classes

5. Suu Kyi was the leader of a group that wanted **democracy**.
   ○ a. government by a king   ○ b. government run by the people
   ○ c. government run by soldiers

6. The leaders of Myanmar feared Suu Kyi's **influence**.
   ○ a. power over people   ○ b. having a lot of money
   ○ c. ability to speak clearly

Read and Remember

■ Find the best ending for each sentence. Fill in the circle next to it.

1. Suu Kyi believed that the people of Burma wanted
   ○ a. better jobs.   ○ b. stronger leaders.   ○ c. freedom.

2. Suu Kyi returned to Burma in 1988 in order to
   ○ a. lead a march.   ○ b. care for her mother.   ○ c. get married.

3. Myanmar's leaders were
   ○ a. pleased with Suu Kyi.   ○ b. helped by Suu Kyi.
   ○ c. afraid of Suu Kyi.

4. Suu Kyi became the leader of the
   ○ a. military government.   ○ b. National League of Democracy.
   ○ c. Nobel Prize committee.

5. Suu Kyi won the Nobel Peace Prize while she was
   ○ a. under house arrest.   ○ b. living in Britain.   ○ c. in the U.S.

Think and Apply—Drawing Conclusions

■ Finish each sentence by writing the best answer.

1. Suu Kyi came to stay with her mother in 1988 because _____

   _____

2. Suu Kyi did not like Myanmar's government because _____

   _____

3. Military leaders refused to accept election results because _____

   _____

4. Suu Kyi did not leave the country when she was given the chance

   because _____

Glossary

absolutely, page 69
Absolutely means completely. He was absolutely sure that he wanted to play on the baseball team.

accused, page 73
If you accuse a person of something, you charge him or her of doing something wrong. The teacher accused her of cheating on the test.

advance, page 48
If you help the progress of something, you advance it. The scientists hoped their work would advance the search for a cure for cancer.

appropriate, page 47
If something is appropriate, it is suitable and proper. It is not appropriate to wear a bathing suit in a nice restaurant.

arrested, page 33
Arrested means held by the police for breaking a law. He was arrested and charged with robbery.

banned, page 49
If something is banned, it is against the law. Smoking is banned in many public places.

barbed-wire, page 27
Barbed-wire is a type of fence with sharp metal points.

basic, page 31
If something is basic, it is important and necessary. Learning to read is a basic part of your education.

bitter, page 40
If someone is bitter, he or she is filled with hate.

brutal, page 80
If someone is brutal, he or she willingly causes pain or suffering. The brutal guard beat the prisoner.

cells, page 19
Cells are the tiny parts of matter that make up all living things. Red blood cells carry oxygen to the rest of the body.

challenged, page 69
To challenge is to question whether something is true. She challenged the idea that only boys could run long distances.

classic, page 47
A classic is an excellent book or piece of art. Many of Van Gogh's paintings are considered classics.

communities, page 27
Communities are groups of people who live and work together.

compared, page 14
Compared means studied to see how things are alike or different.

concerned, page 27
To be concerned means to be worried or troubled about something.

conclusions, page 13
Conclusions are decisions or opinions reached after thinking about something. Lucy reached the conclusion that she would never be a dancer.

concrete, page 30
Concrete is a hardened mixture of sand, clay, and water used in sidewalks, buildings, and bridges.

conditions, page 25
Conditions are the way things are or the state of things. Working conditions in the factory were very bad.

contact, page 75
If you are in touch with someone, you have contact with that person. When Paul moved to Alaska, he lost contact with all his old friends.

cot, page 44
A cot is a narrow bed. Most cots can be folded up.

criminals, page 27
Criminals are people who have broken the law.

criticized, page 45
If you criticize something, you find fault with it.

death, page 48
Death is the end of life.

declaring, page 56
If you declare something, you announce or say it strongly. She declared that she was running for class president.

democracy, page 82
Democracy is a form of government that is run by the people who live under it.

deserved, page 31
To deserve means to be worthy of or to have a right to something.

despair, page 77
Despair means loss of hope. John was filled with despair when he saw the grades on his report card.

desperately, page 77
Desperately means having a great need to do or have something. He desperately needed food and shelter.

dignity, page 31
Dignity is the sense of having honor and self worth.

drill, page 11
To drill means to teach by making someone do the same thing again and again.

drugs, page 19
Drugs are medicines that are used to treat sicknesses.

eccentric, page 61
If someone is eccentric, he or she is different or odd in some way. Everyone thought the woman who wore nothing but purple, was very eccentric.

education, page 2
Education is the knowledge or skills gained at school. Education often trains a person for a certain kind of job.

elections, page 82
People choose leaders by voting in elections. An election is held every two years to choose the mayor.

element, page 6
An element is one of the materials from which all other things are made. Carbon and oxygen are two common elements.

encouragement, page 31
If you receive hope or courage from someone or something, you have received encouragement.

energy, page 15
Energy is the ability to do work. Heat and light are two kinds of energy.

equipment, page 20
Equipment is tools or supplies used for a certain purpose. Camping equipment is sold in that store.

evil, page 27
An evil person is someone who is very bad and harms others.

expressed, page 81
To express means to put into words. He expressed his anger by writing a letter to the editor.

foreign, page 40
Foreign means outside a person's own country. Sally speaks two foreign languages.

generation, page 67
A generation is one step on the ladder that goes from grandparent to parent to child, and so on. This photograph shows four generations of the Webster family.

genes, page 69
Genes are the tiny bits of matter that carry qualities from parents to their young. This gene determines hair color.

genetics, page 66
Genetics is the science that studies how certain features or qualities are passed from parents to children.

germs, page 19
Germs are small living things that can enter the body and cause sicknesses.

getaway, page 52
Getaway means escape. He was driving the getaway car for the bank robbers.

gloomy, page 60
If something is gloomy, it is sad or dark. January is a gloomy, rainy month here.

horrible, page 20
If something is horrible, it causes shock and fear.

horrified, page 40
If you are horrified, you are filled with fear and shock.

imaginary, page 63
If something is imaginary, it isn't real.

infections, page 19
Infections are sicknesses caused when harmful things enter the body. I got an infection when I cut my hand on a rusty piece of metal.

influence, page 82
Influence is the power someone has to produce an effect on other people.

innocent, page 53
If you are innocent, you have done nothing wrong.

interrupted, page 2
To interrupt means to break in while someone else is talking.

journalist, page 63
Someone who writes for a newspaper or magazine is called a journalist.

kernels, page 67
Kernels are the whole seed or grain of corn, wheat, or other plants. You can see the kernels on an ear of corn.

labor, page 39
Labor means work. A labor camp is a place where people are forced to work.

laboratory, page 18
A laboratory is a room where science experiments are done.

literature, page 40
Literature is writing that has value and meaning. Shakespeare's plays are some of the world's greatest literature.

material, page 31
If something is material, it can be touched and measured.

mathematicians, page 46
Mathematicians are people who work with numbers.

mathematics, page 11
Mathematics is the study of numbers.

medical, page 18
Medical means having to do with medicine.

memories, page 63
Memories are people or things remembered from the past. One of Anne's best memories was her vacation in Spain.

memorize, page 11
To memorize something means to learn it by heart.

military, page 80
Military means having to do with the armed forces. Military leaders took over the country.

miracle, page 21
A miracle is something wonderful and amazing that can't be completely explained.

miserable, page 6
If something is miserable, it is run-down and not worth much. The miserable, old house was torn down.

mold, page 20
Mold is a furry growth that may appear on food or damp surfaces. We threw the bread out because it had mold on it.

motionless, page 77
Motionless means without movement. The cat sat motionless, watching the bird.

nonviolent, page 83
Nonviolent means peaceful or not violent. The protest was nonviolent in spite of the strong feelings between the two groups.

novel, page 38
A novel is a book about people who are not real and events that did not really happen. *Tom Sawyer* is a well–known novel.

numb, page 75
Numb means losing all feeling. The hikers' feet grew numb after an hour of walking in the snow.

observers, page 57
Observers are people who watch something.

officials, page 12
Officials are people who are in charge of something.

offspring, page 66
Offspring are the young produced by animals or plants. Elephants produce only one offspring at a time.

outspoken, page 25
If you are outspoken, you are open and honest.

overjoyed, page 35
If someone is overjoyed, he or she is very happy.

painful, page 27
If something is painful, it causes pain.

physics, page 6
Physics is the science that studies matter and energy.

praised, page 83
To praise means to speak highly of someone. The coach praised the team for working well together.

protest, page 33
A protest is a meeting where people show by speeches or actions that they are against something.

protesters, page 80
Protesters are people who gather to speak or act out against something.

published, page 77
To publish means to print a magazine, newspaper, or book and to offer it for sale.

radiation, page 5
Radiation is energy that is given off in waves. X-rays are one form of radiation.

referred, page 45
To refer to something means to direct attention to it. She referred to her father in the speech.

refugees, page 26
Refugees are people who leave their homes in search of safety.

relative, page 14
If something is relative, it has meaning only when judged against something else. What you think of as cold weather is relative to what part of the country you are from.

represented, page 40
To represent means to be a symbol of or to stand for something. The flag represented freedom to the soldiers.

research, page 5
Research is the careful study of a certain subject to find out more about it.

researcher, page 67
A researcher is someone who studies one subject. After many years, the researchers found a way to prevent polio.

sane, page 77
If you are sane, you have a clear, healthy mind. Sane is the opposite of crazy.

smuggle, page 74
To smuggle means to send or carry something secretly. The prisoner's brother smuggled a message to him.

solitude, page 63
Solitude is the state of being alone.

stationary, page 13
If something is stationary, it does not move. Flagpoles are usually stationary.

strict, page 11
If you are strict, you insist that all rules be followed carefully.

struggle, page 27
A struggle is something that requires great effort.

style, page 63
Style is a certain manner of saying or doing something.

superstitious, page 62
If you are superstitious, you believe that certain things cause good luck or bad buck. The superstitious boy was worried when he stepped on the crack in the sidewalk.

supporters, page 56
Supporters are people who believe in a certain cause.

targeting, page 54
If you target something, you aim at it.

terrorist, page 54
Terrorist attacks are actions meant to frighten, hurt, or kill others.

ton, page 6
A ton equals 2,000 pounds.

tragedy, page 41
If something very sad or terrible happens, it is called a tragedy. The earthquake that shook Mexico City was a great tragedy.

traitor, page 54
A traitor is a person who acts against his or her own country or people.

traits, page 66
A trait is a feature or quality of a living thing. Red hair is a common trait in our family.

translating, page 40
Translating means changing something from one language into another language.

treason, page 49
Treason is when someone has helped the enemies of his or her country.

tribute, page 77
A tribute is something which is given to show respect. The principal gave Susan the award as a tribute to all her hard work.

triumphs, page 31
Triumphs are great successes.

tropical, page 61
Tropical means having to do with the area near the equator. Tropical towns are warm all-year long.

turmoil, page 81
Turmoil means great confusion. The small town was in turmoil after the hurricane.

units, page 69
Units are single things that are part of a larger group.

university, page 2
A university is a school of higher learning that trains people for many different kinds of jobs.

uranium, page 5
Uranium is a silver-colored metal that gives off special rays.

violence, page 52
Violence is the use of great force to do harm.

visas, page 38
Visas are official papers allowing people to travel in another country.

vivid, page 62
Vivid means lively and active. Her vivid description of the tornado was exciting.

zone, page 55
A zone is an area used for a special purpose.

Keeping Score

1. Count the number of correct answers you have for each activity.
2. Write these numbers in the boxes in the chart.
3. Ask your teacher to give you a score (maximum score 5) for Write Your Ideas.
4. Add up the numbers to get a final score.

Stories	Vocabulary	Read and Remember	Think and Apply	Write Your Ideas	Score
Marie Curie					/18
Albert Einstein					/25
Alexander Fleming					/20
Emily Greene Balch					/20
Albert Luthuli					/18
Nelly Sachs					/19
Alexander Solzhenitsyn					/20
Betty Williams and Mairead Corrigan					/15
Gabriel García Márquez					/18
Barbara McClintock					/18
Wole Soyinka					/20
Aung San Suu Kyi					/18

Answer Key

Marie Curie — Pages 2–9

Vocabulary Skill Builder:
Part A: 1. uranium, 2. radiation, 3. elements, 4. research
Part B: 1-d, 2-a, 3-f, 4-b, 5-e, 6-c
Read and Remember: 2, 3, 5
Write Your Ideas: Answers will vary.

Albert Einstein — Pages 10–17

Vocabulary Skill Builder:
Part A: Answers will vary.
Part B: 1-c, 2-a, 3-c, 4-c, 5-a, 6-c, 7-c
Read and Remember:
1. Einstein felt sorry for the soldiers.
2. Einstein asked too many questions.
3. They helped and encouraged him.
4. His ideas made people look at the world in a new way.
5. It would stop ticking.
Think and Apply—Fact or Opinion?
1-F, 2-O, 3-O, 4-F, 5-O, 6-F, 7-F, 8-O, 9-O, 10-F

Alexander Fleming — Pages 18–23

Vocabulary Skill Builder: *Across:*
5. medical, 6. drugs, 7. miracle, 9. laboratory, 10. infections
Down: 1. mold, 2. cells, 3. equipment, 4. horrible, 8. germs
Read and Remember: 1-a, 2-b, 3-c, 4-c, 5-a
Write Your Ideas: Answers will vary.

Emily Greene Balch — Pages 24–29

Vocabulary Skill Builder:
Part A: 1-g, 2-f, 3-a, 4-e, 5-c, 6-d, 7-b
Part B: Answers will vary.
Read and Remember: 1-c, 2-b, 3-b, 4-b, 5-b
Think and Apply—Finding the Sequence: 4, 3, 5, 1, 2

Albert Luthuli — Pages 30–37

Vocabulary Skill Builder:
Part A: 1-a, 2-a, 3-c, 4-b, 5-a
Part B: 1. basic, 2. protests, 3. arrested, 4. overjoyed, 5. encouragement
Read and Remember: 1, 4, 5
Write Your Ideas: Answers will vary.

Nelly Sachs — Pages 38–43

Vocabulary Skill Builder: 1. visas, 2. foreign, 3. horrified, 4. literature, 5. tragedy, 6. bitter, 7. represented, 8. labor, 9. novel, 10. translating
Code words—A GREAT POET
Read and Remember:
1. The Nazis sent millions of German Jews to death camps.
2. Lagerlöf went to the Swedish royal family to get visas for Nelly and her mother.
3. Nelly's poems were about the death camps and the suffering of the Jews.
4. The images of dust and smoke represent death.
5. She believed her words were for all Jews, not just Israelis.
Think and Apply—Cause and Effect: Answers may vary. Here are some examples.
1. Nelly had read Lagerlöf's novel and was very impressed by it.
2. she had learned that she would soon be sent to a labor camp.
3. the German language had been used by the Nazis to sentence many people to death.
4. she needed to express her feelings about the horrible things that had happened to her people.

Alexander Solzhenitsyn   Pages 44–51

Vocabulary Skill Builder:
Part A: 1-b, 2-e, 3-f, 4-a, 5-g, 6-d, 7-c
Part B: Answers will vary.
Read and Remember: 1-c, 2-a, 3-b, 4-a, 5-b

Write Your Ideas:
Answers will vary.

Betty Williams & Mairead Corrigan   Pages 52–59

Vocabulary Skill Builder: *Across:*
2. terrorist, 3. getaway, 4. supporters, 8. violence, 9. declaring. *Down:*
1. traitor, 2. targeting, 5. observers, 6. innocent, 7. zone

Read and Remember: 2, 3, 6

Think and Apply—Main Ideas: 1, 4

Gabriel García Márquez   Pages 60–65

Vocabulary Skill Builder: 1. gloomy, 2. vivid, 3. superstitious 4. solitude, 5. eccentric, 6. imaginary, 7. style, 8. journalist, 9. tropical, 10. memories
Code word—LITERATURE

Read and Remember
1. His parents left Aracataca and did not want to take their son with them.
2. He loved listening to the stories, but he was also frightened by them.
3. Zipaquirá was dark and rainy. Gabriel was far from his family and very lonely.
4. He wanted to escape the loneliness and gloom.
5. They were filled with imaginary events, and most of them dealt with solitude.

Write Your Ideas
Answers will vary.

Barbara McClintock   Pages 66–71

Vocabulary Skill Builder
Part A: 1. researcher, 2. genetics, 3. generation, 4. challenged, 5. genes
Part B: 1-b, 2-c, 3-a, 4-c, 5-a
Read and Remember: 2, 5, 6
Think and Apply—Finding the Sequence: 1, 3, 2, 4, 5

Wole Soyinka   Pages 72–79

Vocabulary Skill Builder: *Across:*
2. motionless, 5. sane, 6. desperately, 9. tribute, 10. published *Down:*
1. contact, 3. smuggle, 4. despair, 7. accused, 8. numb

Read and Remember
1. Gowon believed Soyinka had been working with the Ibos to start a war.
2. Soyinka was a great writer and a good person.
3. His feet grew numb and his skin cracked. But mainly he suffered from lack of contact with the outside world.
4. He used a crow's feather as a pen and toilet paper as writing paper.
5. He wrote poems and a play.

Write Your Ideas: Answers will vary.

Aung San Suu Kyi   Pages 80–85

Vocabulary Skill Builder:
Part A: Answers will vary.
Part B: 1-c, 2-b, 3-b, 4-a, 5-b, 6-a
Read And Remember: 1-c, 2-b, 3-c, 4-b, 5-a
Think and Apply—Drawing Conclusions:
1. her mother was ill.
2. it did not give the Burmese people freedom.
3. they had lost.
4. the military leaders did not agree to meet her demands.